Paul Mealor

STABAT MATER

for solo soprano, SATB divisi chorus and piano

NOVELLO

The first movement of the *Stabat Mater* is for choir only; the piano is tacet.

Duration: *circa* 25 minutes

Order No. NOV292853

Also available for solo soprano, SATB divisi chorus, harp (or piano) and strings
NOV292864 (score).
Parts are available on hire from the publisher.

STABAT MATER

Stabat mater dolorosa
juxta crucem lacrimosa,
dum pendebat filius.

At the cross her station keeping,
stood the mournful mother weeping,
close to her son to the last.

Cujus animam gementem,
contristatam et dolentem,
pertransivit gladius.

Through her heart, his sorrow sharing,
all his bitter anguish bearing,
now at length the sword has passed.

Quis non posset contristari,
Christi matrem contemplari
dolentem cum filio?

Can the human heart refrain
from partaking in her pain,
in that mother's pain untold?

Pro peccatis suæ gentis
vidit Jesum in tormentis
et flagellis subditum.

For the sins of his own nation,
She saw Jesus wracked with torment,
All with scourges rent.

Vidit suum dulcem natum
moriendo desolatum,
dum emisit spiritum.

She beheld her tender child,
Saw him hang in desolation,
Till his spirit forth he sent.

Eia mater, fons amoris,
me sentire vim doloris
fac, ut tecum lugeam.

O thou mother, fount of love,
Touch my spirit from above,
make my heart with thine accord.

Fac ut ardeat cor meum
in amando Christum Deum
ut sibi complaceam.

Make me feel as thou hast felt;
make my soul to glow and melt
with the love of Christ my Lord.

Sancta mater, istud agas,
crucifixi fige plagas
cordi meo valide.

Holy mother, pierce me through,
in my heart each wound renew
of my saviour crucified.

Tui nati vulnerati,
tam dignati pro me pati,
pœnas mecum divide.

Let me share with thee his pain,
who for all my sins was slain,
who for me in torments died.

Virgo virginum præclara,
mihi jam non sis amara,
fac me tecum plangere.

Virgin of all virgins blest,
listen to my fond request:
let me share thy grief divine;

Fac, ut portem Christi mortem,
passionis fac consortem,
et plagas recolere.

Let me, to my latest breath,
in my body bear the death
of that dying son of thine.

Fac me plagis vulnerari,
fac me cruce inebriari,
et cruore filii.

Wounded with his every wound,
steep my soul till it hath swooned,
in his very blood away;

Flammis ne urar succensus,
per te, Virgo, sim defensus
in die judicii.

Be to me, O Virgin, nigh,
lest in flames I burn and die,
in his awful judgment day.

Christe, cum sit hinc exire,
da per matrem me venire
ad palmam victoriæ.

Quando corpus morietur,
fac, ut animæ donetur
paradisi gloria. Amen.

Christ, when thou shalt call me hence,
by thy mother my defence,
by thy cross my victory;

While my body here decays,
may my soul thy goodness praise,
Safe in paradise with thee.

Translation by Edward Caswall
Lyra Catholica (1849)

dedicated, in memoriam, to my grandparents, with love and affection

Stabat Mater

PAUL MEALOR

1. Stabat mater dolorosa

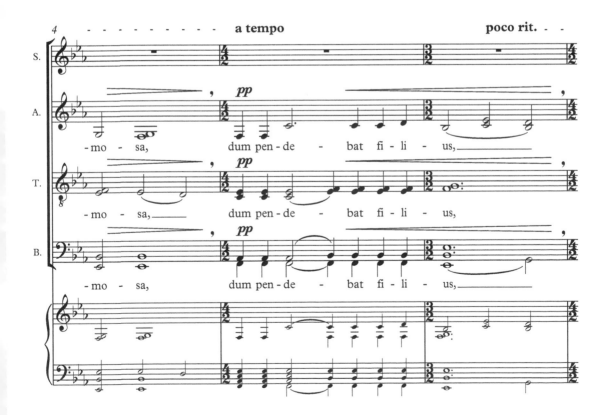

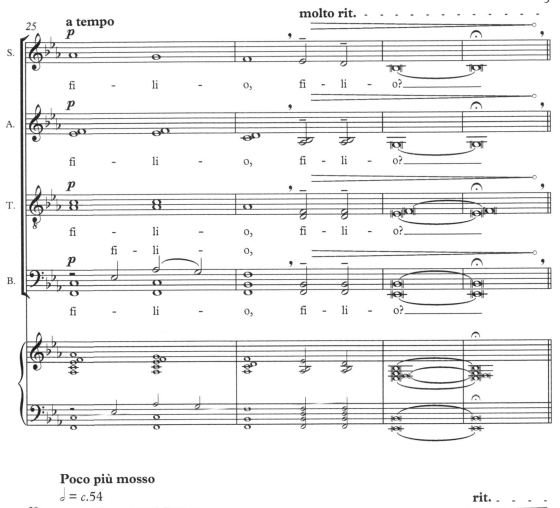

2. Eia mater, fons amoris

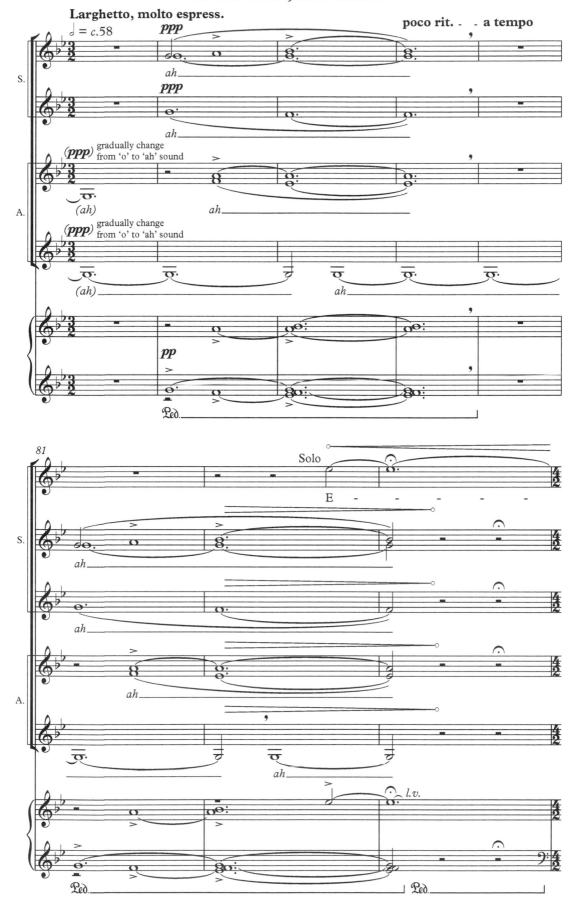

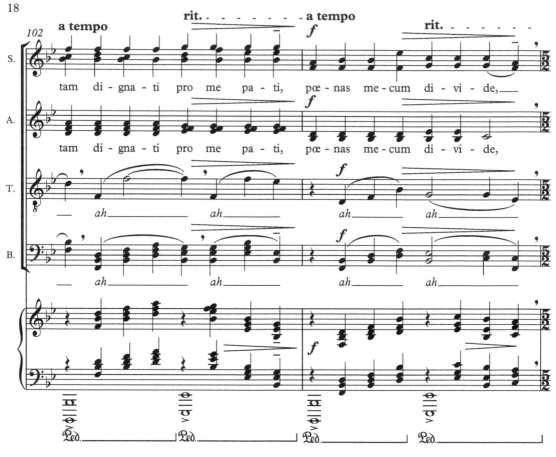

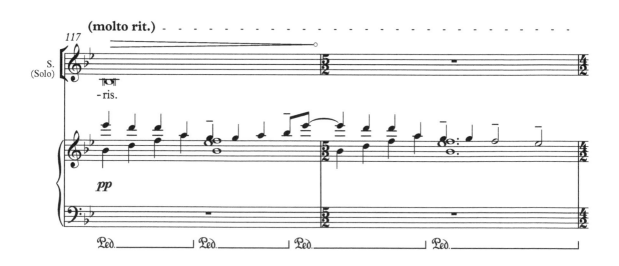

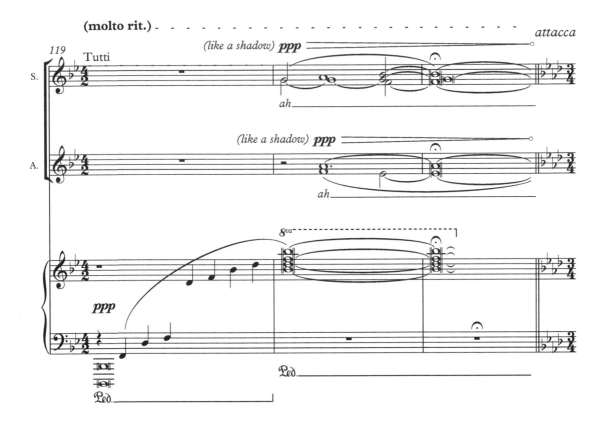

3. Virgo virginum præclara

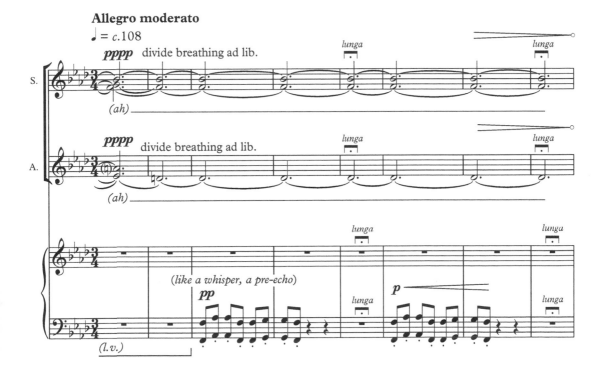

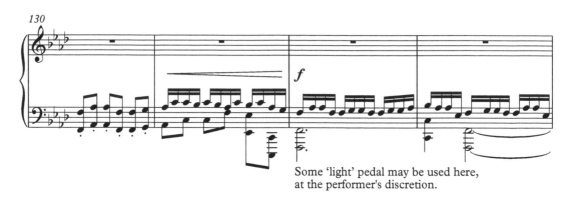

Some 'light' pedal may be used here,
at the performer's discretion.

T. Vir - go vir - gi - num præ - cla - ra, mi - hi jam non

B. Vir - go vir - gi - num præ - cla - ra, mi - hi jam non

T. sis a - mar - a, fac___ me te - cum plan - ge - re.___

B. sis a - mar - a, fac___ me te - cum plan - ge - re.___

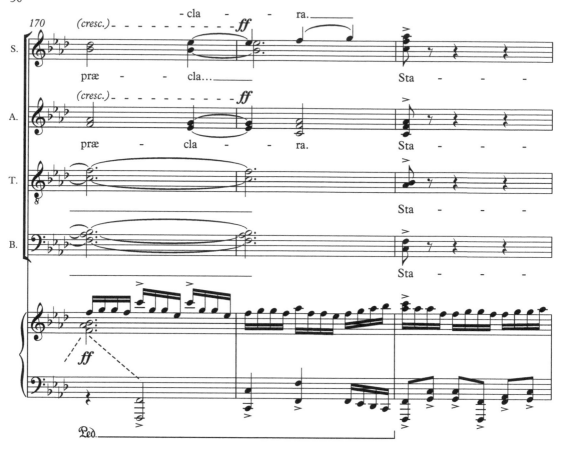

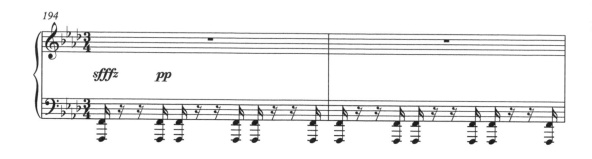

4. Christe, cum sit hinc exire

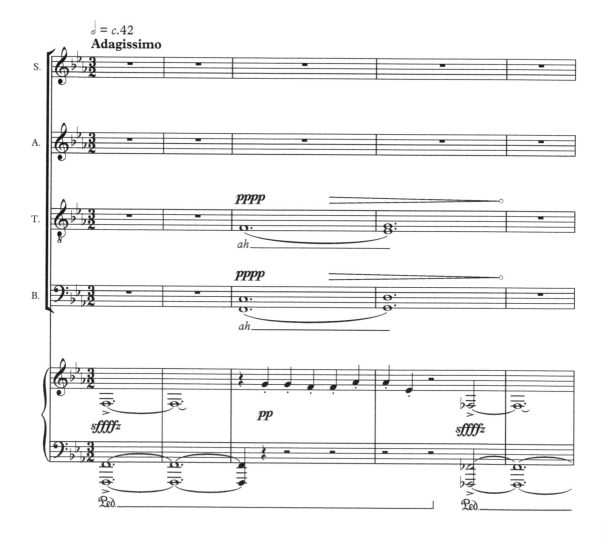

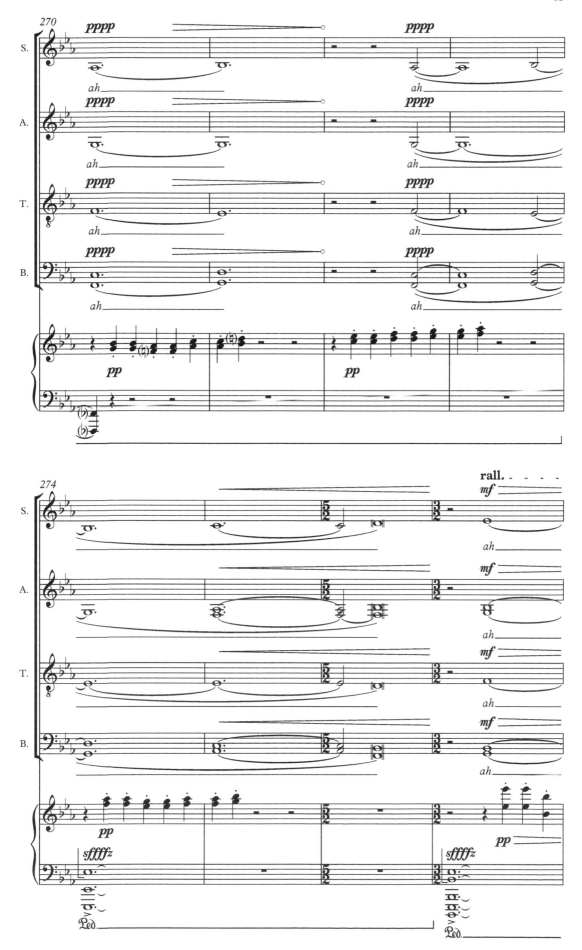

46

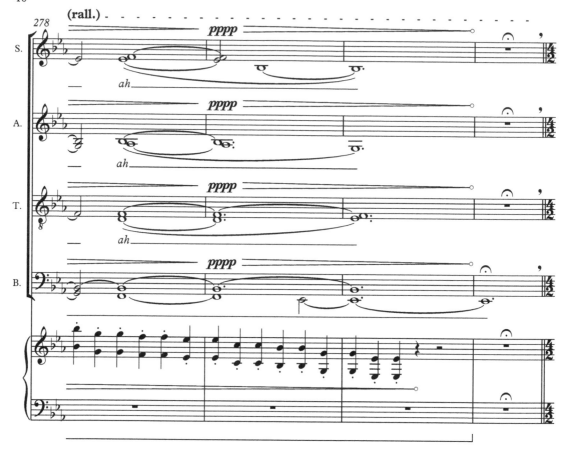

48

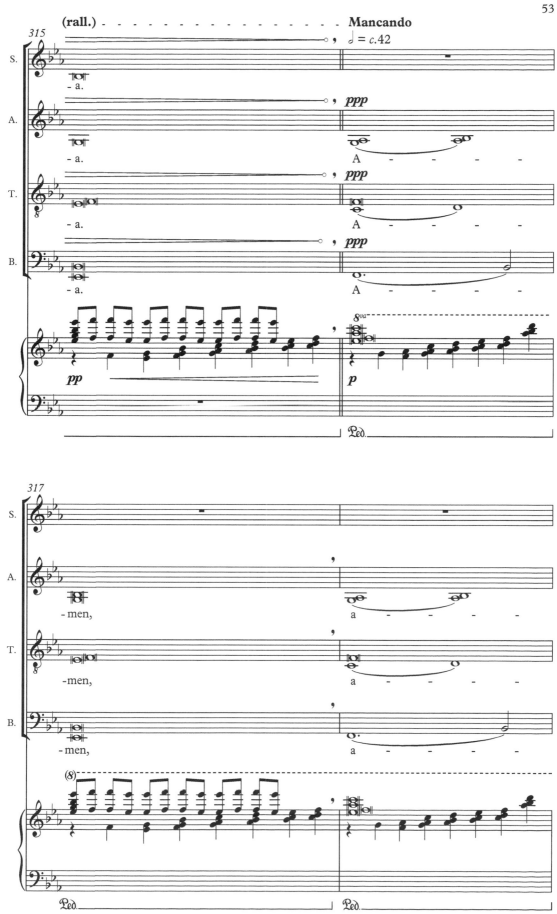

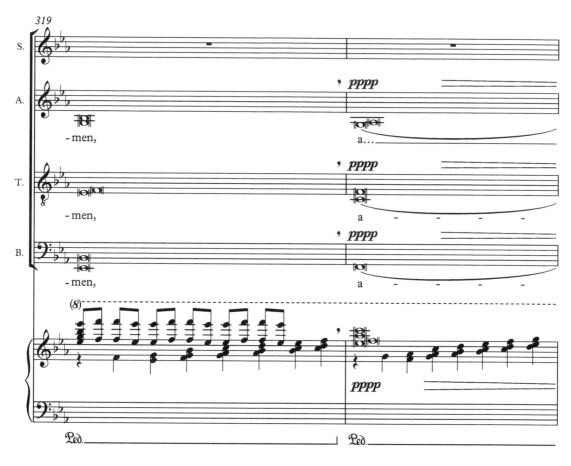

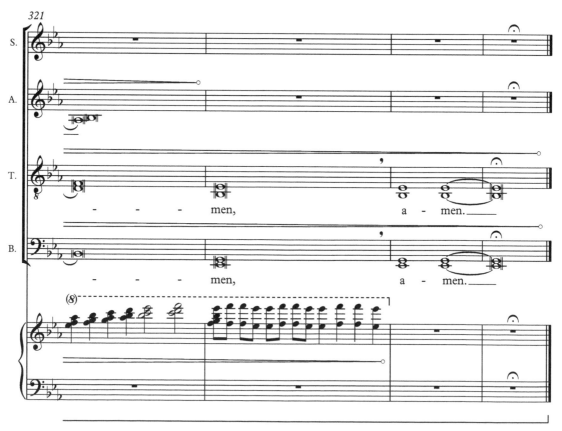